Lost Between Two Worlds

By

Nicholas Ruggiero

Final Chapter by

Logan Campbell

Table of contents

1. Making the choice
2. Three degrees of separation
3. Civilian life acclimating
4. Stories for days
5. Leadership PTSD
6. Lunch
7. Regret, failure, and repeat
8. Defining your existence
9. "It's a bad car crash"

Dedication

This book is dedicated to the woman who stood by me when I didn't stand by her in times of self-destruction, my wife Nicole. You stuck with me when it wasn't easy and for that, I love you always.

Hailey, I see so much of me in you. You are impulsive and passionate which can be a great asset when you learn to utilize it. Know your north and how to always correct your course. Know your worth and always demand it be met. Never let someone tell you who you are and how to be that person.

Emy, I can't put into words how incredibly proud I am of you and what you've witnessed over the past two years. I've watched you grow into someone that has come out of her shell and given the world the real you with no regrets. Never apologize for being you no matter what people accept or don't accept. #MGK4LIFE

Mom and Dad, Always there for me and always ready to pick up the pieces of my life. Mom you've always been the person I can text or call and pour my heart to and not worry about judgment. I hope I've made you proud with these books and what I've done.

Mike, I wouldn't be here and have come this far without you always being there when I need you. The word "Friend" is not fair to call you because you're like a brother to me. Lizpza is lucky to have you in his life.

Denny Proffitt, our paths were supposed to cross and I'm glad I didn't blow off that conference. I'm excited for you to do the great things you're destined to do.

William Young, Thank you for saving my wife's life and being there for her with your books when I wasn't. "The nothing that never happened" continues to save lives and show the side of corrections that people need too.

Ernest Stevens, you will always have a place in these books! Joe, I see you, bro! Ed, thanks again for being willing to give me the honesty that I need and tell me how it is. John, I met you when you were at doorsteps brother, and over the past year, I've watched you take on life and win. I admire your happiness about life and pure and genuine friendship. Thank you for reminding me how to enjoy life.

T.J., Laura, and Alex I love you guys!

Foreword

By

Ret. NYPD Detective Michael Ferrante

Picture this, Hicksville Long Island, 2002. On my way home from working overnight for New York's Finest. I decided, I was going to stop off and visit a high school friend, who was working at his family's dog grooming salon. I see him standing outside. I can see he can't wait to tell me something. "Hey, I want you to meet the guy next store that owns the tattoo shop". "Sure" I say reluctantly. Thinking to myself, I don't want to meet this prick. I'm now starting to crash and just want to go home to get some sleep. A quiet house (no kids and was engaged to be married next month, so no wife either).

Outcomes this mother fucker, "Hey bro what's up, You see Jackass". From that moment my bromance with Nick began. Meeting his incredible, beautiful, big pregnant wife and being there when his daughters were born was amazing.
Nick and Nicole even came to my wedding. Mainly, because they didn't think my wife existed. That was because my routine since that day was to go to work then head over to the tattoo shop. Nick and I would hang out in between and during tattoos. I would be his apprentice and learn from the best….. Nick didn't know it then, and maybe hasn't realized it yet, but those days helped me deal with the job. Having a place to go, laugh and joke around, allowed me to deal with the job and the stress from that day.

When Nick joined Virginia's Police Department, he went from a (Two-Five) security auxiliary to a real Cop (Five-0). I couldn't help to think I was losing my best friend, but I knew his department was getting a great man, who was willing to put everyone ahead of himself.

Fast forward twenty years later I'm now retired from the greatest Police Department in the world and trying to figure out what the next twenty years of my life will be like.

To think now our time in law enforcement has come to an end and we are still continuing our bromance.

As someone who is just starting the journey of life after the job, I'm fortunate to have Nick and this book. Beginning the experience of what it's like after 20 years of service to become a civilian again, is challenging. Being a cop is all I know since I was 18 years old. Majoring in Criminal Justice at St. Johns University, I always wanted to be a cop. I'm thankful I have Nick (good ole Skippy and his trilogy). I hear he may start to write romance novels next, too bad my grandmother isn't alive for that one. She would have been first online to get a signed copy. Nick has been my Ride or Die! He is the one I called after seeing and being a witness to some of the most heinous crimes you can think of. He knew exactly what I was going through and how I felt being a cop himself and he talked me through some really tough times, and for that, I am forever in his debt.

Whether you aged out, medically cleared out, or forced out, we are all in the same boat, trying to figure out how we get by without, roll call, sleepless days, the laughs, jokes, and being needed on a level many never get to experience. Seeing more of the decent side of the human race, rather than years of seeing the human race at its worst. How will I get by without being in charge of something? Not being able to help the people who needed my help.

Transition to civilian life is not easy. The last twenty years were more than just a job. It was a way of life. A way of thinking. It controlled me and my everyday living. I spent more time at work dealing with cases than I did with my own family. The job consumed me.

This book really hits home. Nick talks about being "LOST BETWEEN TWO WORLDS" the struggles of everyday life not being "ON THE JOB". He acknowledges the loss of not getting that adrenal rush of responding to a call, the thrill of throwing on lights and sirens to help the people who are in need of police intervention. He also shares his experience of watching people on the streets and knowing there are perps out there, but he cannot do anything about it. He speaks about how home life is different. Interaction with his family is different. All-around life is different.

To end, this book will share Nick's experiences on how crossing over to civilian life will take some time and some getting used to, but in the end, we were born to be cops. It's in our blood and we will forever be cops. Be safe watch each other's back. We all sign out together!!

Ret. NYPD Detective Michael Ferrante

Chapter 1
"Making the choice"

One of the hardest choices I've ever made was leaving a profession that I loved and wanted to do since I was a kid. Not only was it hard, but it was twice as hard cause I did it twice.

The first time I did it was because I was under extreme stress and in a hostile work environment that my department did nothing about. Furthermore, I started to feel like my mental health didn't matter to them. I started to have my home life destroyed and to make matters worse it was making me physically ill.

At first, I made the "soft decision" to leave. This is where you put a half-assed effort into looking for something else, but deep down you know you're full of shit and won't follow through. You start applying for jobs that are ridiculous or you're not qualified for. Things like a Mars robot operator or CEO of Google. It's just a way of saying, "Fuck you" to your department.

I did that for a few months until a response from a job that was paying a stupid amount of money called me for an interview. I took the bait.

When I went on the interview it was amazing to have people at the edge of their seats in awe of what I did for my ungrateful department. I heard things that I've never heard like "You're talented" "You have a great skill set that we love".

At the end of my first interview, I was really on cloud nine but I had some guilt. I felt like I was betraying my agency and the people in it. At the time I was a Sergeant in charge of some of the finest officers my agency had to offer. I mentored some of these people and helped them get promoted. I attended their weddings, kids' birthdays, and had them over my house for BBQs and kids parties.

It weighed on me heavily for a long time. I intentionally didn't call back the Human Resource Manager hoping it would go away, but it didn't. She made me feel like my knowledge and skills could be better used at another agency. When we started to talk about salary I made up some ridiculous figure to throw them off, but that didn't work. They agreed to it and I accepted.

Giving my notice was tough. On one hand, I was happy for the pain to go away and show my department that I was serious. On the other hand, I wanted my chief to beg me to stay or say, "I'll fix it, we fucked up please don't go". Instead, the prick acted like I didn't even matter. He acted like I was telling him that the copier was out of paper. Hearing his indignant attitude set me off and the filter I tried to have gone out the window. I can tell he didn't want to speak with me or answer any further questions so I left his office.

I remember walking to my car and sobbing for a while. Not because of the way he spoke to me but because I spent 14.5 years of my life going into that building and giving 110%. I missed my kid's entire childhood for that place and that cock sucker couldn't even show empathy or even attempt to keep me. He acted like I did something wrong and that I was an asshole for leaving.

I remember calling my wife and immediately she knew it didn't go well. She asked me what happened but I could formulate a sentence because I was still in shock, angry, and upset. I was able to say to her that when I went into his office I almost pulled back my resignation, but not even five minutes into talking to him I knew it was the right choice.

After you make that decision to leave comes a flurry of emotions. Happiness, sadness, anger, and others. Cock suckers that you pretended to get along with, you no longer have to. I remember walking down the hall and saying, "You're cool, you're an asshole, you're a cock sucker, You're a scammer". Roll calls were great because

I said what I wanted or what people were thinking and couldn't say.

Alone, I was sad and depressed because people I respected all the years I worked there turned their backs and acted like I was a traitor. Some wouldn't even talk to me.

One of my fellow Sergeants threw me a going-away luncheon. Not a lot of people showed up which hurt but that didn't matter because my wife and kids were able to attend. Most of the people that came were mostly interested in the food. Fucking cops love free food.

What happened after I left and went to my new job happens to a lot of folks when they leave law enforcement. We'll talk about it in this book and why after all that I went back for more abuse. I can only compare it to a domestic violence relationship.

I learned that deciding to leave was the easy part, it's keeping the decision to stay away that's the hard part. Fighting the inner you not to return because of multiple reasons. My advice is to stay gone! I talked to a lot of people that left law enforcement about this and they all have gone through it which is, "Did I make the right choice by leaving the cult?".

I tell you this because if you're in that stage now where you're thinking about leaving, this book is important. We'll discuss what comes with the choice to leave and the emotions that will happen when you do leave. Only you can make that decision to leave. Matter of fact I highly recommend it be solely your decision. I say this because you will grow to resent your friend or loved one that pushed you away if you weren't ready. Don't do that to them. Ultimately you'll know when it's time to hang it up. Don't do it for the wrong reason, and more importantly don't stay because you think the department can't function without you, cause trust me they can.

Chapter 2

"Three degrees of separation"

The first part is deciding it's time to roll out. Whatever your reasons such as retirement or resigning it's tough. The longer you're in it the tougher the degrees of separation are. I call this the three degrees of separation.

The first degree of separation is joy or happiness. This is an emotion that fuck's with you. You're happy or relieved because whatever the reason for your departure, it's now over. You start to think about how awesome it's going to be and all the things that you're going to do that you couldn't while at your old department or in the profession in general. In the next chapter, we're going to talk about that in detail because it's important.

This first degree is great for your family because they've been on the ride-along your entire career so to them this is awesome. They get to have a life again and you as you, but it's not you.

Your brain goes into this trance in the happy stage. It blocks out thinking about the other emotions that are coming and revels in the now of just being out. For me leaving law enforcement was out of anger and betrayal from my former agency. For a while anytime I would think about the fact that I left the thought of "Fuck those clowns" would come up. Deep down that wasn't the real feeling or emotion I was having. Instead, I was lying to myself to support my decision. Furthermore, anytime my wife would ask me if I was happy I'd lie and say, "Fuck yea, fuck that job." Again, in reality, I missed it, and fairly quickly I slipped into the second degree of separation.

The second degree of separation is the tough one because this is where a lot of people that leave law enforcement go back. I fell into this trap. Regret. When I left law enforcement and after the fake happiness faded was when I started to regret the decision. All I can think of was the people I left at my old department and how I was a valuable asset to the department. Just writing that made me want to throw up. More because it's such bullshit but we buy into it. I bought into it big time. While I was at my new high-paying job away from my old agency all I could think of is how the agency couldn't be surviving without me which is nuts.

This emotion is dangerous because it's like a domestic violence scenario. We see it time after time on the job. The abuse over and over again becomes second nature until we accept it. The long hours to chase that carrot or the ability to make a lot of money through overtime at the sacrifice of your family.

When you leave the job it's like a breakup and depending on your length of time on the job or devotion to the job the breakup is severe. For me, the bbreakupwas like a divorce after 20 years. I had revolved my entire life around my agency and my position within it. I believed that my position defined my existence. Typing that sentence almost made me barf. Looking at it now I realize how insane that is, but at the time I was convinced that I had to return because something was missing and my self-worth was wrapped up in that job. The problem with that theory is not knowing when enough is enough. I've seen people leave and come back and destroy their mental health even more. When you know it's time to go, it's time to go. Stick to your guns and trust your instinct. Don't buy into that domestic mentality, "It'll get better, it's only like this because I'm not trying hard enough". It's bullshit…

The third degree of separation is acceptance of being out of law enforcement or changing departments. Later in this book, I'll talk about some of the things that you'll experience about leaving law enforcement altogether. Some of you reading this that retired or left law enforcement altogether will understand.

The acceptance of leaving the job takes time for some. I was/am one of those people. The longer you've been in this job the longer it takes for the acceptance part.

I remember the first day I wasn't a cop anymore was weird and I felt off. I went from carrying a gun to work every day, to not carrying guns. I went from an elevated level of alertness to being one of the sheep in the pasture. Let's make it clear that I'm still at an alertness level but not at the level I was before. What I mean is when you're a cop and off duty, you continue to scan, observe, and strategize. Even at Chucky Cheese, I remember looking around and picking out potential shitheads and scanning for exits if shit went down. After leaving the job it switches to being a good witness, getting your family out, and surviving.

I'm not saying when you leave law enforcement you turn into a coward and hide like a baby. I'm saying that you have to accept your new role as a civilian. You should be using the skills you learned to save your family and however many innocents you feel like it. In the "Cop" mode your focus is to save them all and lay down the lead if you have to. You can't do that like you were allowed to because you're not protected like you were. Legal expenses alone as a civilian with no union coverage are enough to make you want to not get involved. If you're reading this and you say, "Fuck that, I'll lay down fire and deal with that shit later". Kudos to you and it's commendable, but I'll drop some wisdom on you to think about. If you think prosecutors will burn you at the stake for a legit line of duty shooting while being a cop, what do you think they'll do to a former cop involved in a public shooting? I'll tell you... Remember in Pulp Fiction the Gimp scene? Yea that scene… That's pretty much how it'll be during the trial and while you're in jail during trial. If you haven't noticed prosecutors lately are public defenders with their jerseys inside out…

You need to embrace the fact that you're out and you made it safely. This degree of separation is also tough on your family. They'll have to endure your weird schedule adjustment even though you're out of the profession. If you worked midnights it's going to take time to get your body back to being a normal human being who's not drinking Monster drinks and eating beef jerky at 0300hrs. Having Mom or Dad at the dinner table will be an adjustment for the kids. In the next chapter, we'll talk about that more in detail.

Part of the last degree of separation also comes with dealing with people shit-talking the police around you. It's hard to not want to grab a baseball bat and crown them now that you're out of law enforcement. As fun as it would seem, fight that urge. One of the hardest things is to be a law enforcement public defender for me. I would see a Facebook or Twitter post about how all cops suck and "Defund" the police and would want to throw my phone.

Part of accepting the exit from the profession is to also accept the fact that you're not included in those remarks or solutions. Yea it sucks but that's one of the degrees of separation, accepting the fact you're not the police, you're someone who calls the police now. Now, the way to resolve this issue if it is one for you is to help your former brothers and sisters by volunteering your time with pro-law enforcement organizations like #webackblue, Rocks for LEO's, Code 1 Wellness, or any other legitimate entity helping the ones still on the battlefield. I've worked with each one of these listed and these are some of the most dedicated people trying to help law enforcement.

Chapter 3

"Civilian life acclamation"

I'd have to say acclimating to civilian life after leaving law enforcement is tough. I've touched on it in the prior chapters but this part is important to pay attention to.

After leaving law enforcement the acclimation period is different for each person. I've spoken to some of my friends that have left the job and they've been able to acclimate pretty easily with, no issues. If that's you, great! You still should listen to this advice and absorb it.

If you weren't in therapy while on the job then this is a great time to start. You'll want to talk to someone about your prior encounters as a cop and some of the dark shit you've seen. Unless you were a paper pusher and suffer from Xerox PTSD. I remember leaving law enforcement and for a while having some very vivid nightmares. All through my law enforcement career I never had issues sleeping. I once worked a horrible homicide when I was on midnights, came home, and went right to bed. After I left law enforcement it was like the flood gates opened up and all the bad shit I witnessed wanted to have movie time every night while I tried to sleep. At first, I thought something was wrong and that maybe this was a much larger issue, but after speaking with my therapist (see this is why you should have one) she let me know it's very common in retired law enforcement and military personnel. The brain-like to suppress these horrible images and events so that you can go on day after day and maintain your sanity. Your brain files these memories away in what's called a "Do later" file. When you leave it's time to "Do later" and deal with it.

When I go to conferences or talk to guests for my podcast I like to ask, "Since leaving law enforcement, how are you sleeping?". I like to compare and see what the other former LEO's have sleeping issues. Believe it or not, it's a large number of people have issues. They chalk it up to just bad sleep or an odd day, but when I explain to them the cause they get it.

Part of acclimating to civilian life is dealing with the hate of law enforcement but on the civilian side. I spoke briefly about it in the last chapter but this is a little more in-depth.

When I left law enforcement one of the hardest things was to separate myself from the job when listening to anti-cop idiots talk or Facebook warriors go one about how they would do a better job but can't come up from mom's basement. What was interesting was discovering that my voice counts again and my freedom of speech was back. As you know, once we take that oath and adorn that beautiful badge our freedom to say what we want not only on duty but off duty is taken away. How many times have we seen officers go on a tirade on social media just to be crushed by command staff for saying what's true, but not allowed to?

I remember the first time this degree of separation kicked in. I was pulling into Walmart which I highly recommend you don't do till you've been out of the job for at least six months. This car cut me off to take a parking spot I was tactically backing into. This fuck nut had some choice words for me because I was shaking my head. After all, in my old agency I was written up for two off duty disagreements (One was warranted and deserved a no-no talk, the other was my dickhead Sergeant trying to act tough cause he was a paper bitch). Initially, I was conditioned and just kept quiet until a light bulb went off that I was a free man. Free to display my critique of this human piece of shit with no ramifications. Now I tell you this not to encourage you to drag someone out of their car and beat the snot out of them but to point out that it felt good to be able to be human again and show emotion and point out how this gentleman was a fuck head.

As I drove away from that Walmart trip it sunk in that I was civilian now. Sad? Yes, a little but I forgot how much our off-duty life is affected by the job. More now than ever when everyone had a camera and departments are putting officers on spit roasts for the dumbest shit. I've spoken to other cops who have left the job and they have shared similar stories. One officer at a speaking engagement I did share one about his kids. He brought up a great point about how we're conditioned from the academy, field training, and on the street to Ask, Tell, and Make. With law enforcement, there is no negotiating a lawful order. I'm going to ask you to do what I say, I'm going to tell you to do what I ask you to, and then I'm going to make you do what I tell you to do.

When you leave law enforcement that's not the case anymore. You can't go into Jiffy Lub and ask Carl to use 10w40, tell Carl to use 10w40, and then go under the car and physically make Carl 10w40. Doesn't work for that anymore folks. Wish in some cases it did but no go.

This officer shared with me that he had a hard time with his twins once he went to civilian life. He was in constant "Cop" mode with his kids with the ask, tell, and make. He wasn't aware of what he was doing until his wife said, "You can't treat the kids like perps on the street, they don't understand that". It's good to have someone that can see what you're doing and help you avoid those land mines.

Part of civilian acclimation also is adapting from hyper vigilance to the observer. We've been conditioned to always be at heightened alert from where we sit at restaurants, scanning for potential threats to making exit plans in our heads for a possible active shooter. Don't lose this skill, but understand your new role as observer and reporter. This is something that a lot of really great proactive police officers struggle with at retirement or leaving the profession. You're conditioned to be Riggs from Lethal Weapon and now you're Arnold from Kindergarten Cop. Take time to decompress and understand if shit hits the fan get your family out and be a good observer. I'm not telling you to run away from a threat if you want to fly your hero flag high, but remember your family comes first for real this time.

Chapter 4

"Stories for days"

Cops love telling stories, especially to each other while on duty. These stories usually start small and get larger and larger to one-up each other. The best thing about being in law enforcement and telling these stories is that you can all relate to each other. No one gets offended (typically) about how descriptive you get and how vulgar.

When you transfer into civilian life those stories need to be told with some reserve. These folks typically have no clue about shit we see and deal with. A lot of the civilian world takes what they see on LivePD or COPS and thinks it's all foot chases, car chases, and dealing with stupid funny shit. It is but they don't understand the dark side of the job so when you shed light on it com toes the stares and gasps.

I remember going into the civilian job world and working with folks that weren't used to those types of stories. I quickly learned that some of the juicy stories are better kept between me and my cop buddies. Some folks aren't prepared or wired to receive the type of things we've seen and done in the course of keeping order and chaos in check.

In one instance a co-worker at my current job asked me what the worst homicide scene I've ever seen was. To my fellow cops, this is where you crack your knuckle, lean bac,k and say, "Well, hold onto your fucking hat fella boy to I got a story to tell you". Having that question asked from folks in the civilian world gives us a false sense of connection. What I mean by that is that we think they want to hear it but they're not prepared for the shock and horror that loaded question comes with.

Considering myself a pretty good cop storyteller I remember starting my story with the, "We got a call to a shit hole building that we always have problems at". Not realizing that to us this is normal, we base locations on the job with problems. If you see a problem address pop up on the screen your first reaction is, "Fuck, this fucking place again. Why can't they just bulldoze this fucking shit hole and save us all time". You're probably shaking your head agreeing.

As I told my cop war story I can see the co-worker had a look of confusion and disgust which I wasn't use to because most of the time we tell these stories to each other as we gleefully bask in the similarity and similarity to each other stories. We also add to each other's stories like, "Did it smell like shit? Tell me he was naked?". It's almost like and an episode of "Friends" but for cops. Later we'll talk about how this is a form of mental health coping with PTSD.

So, back to my Stephen King thriller story with my co-worker. I get to the part where the homicide was a very violent domestic that resulted in the beheading of a female victim and a child. Yea, really gruesome shit. As I told the story the look of horror now overtook my co-worker. Now, you've heard the term "Know your audience"? Yea, I should of because this person was not prepared for this Rob Zombie Friday the 13th type thriller. To make matters worse I included the gory details of smell, blood spatter, and rage involved to carry out this gruesome double murder.

At the end of my Oscar-worthy story, my co-worker looked at me and said, "Wow, how did YOU survive that?". I was shocked at the question because we don't quantify things like that. It's a job and someone has to go clean up the dark and dirty things humans do to each other.

It made me realize that all of these scenes in my bag of war stories were pieces of my soul that were chipped away over time. Your stories are little souvenirs of things that slowly took over your mental health without you knowing. What we once considered "war stories" are now little glimpses of why we're fucked up.

I will tell you in the civilian world after law enforcement and in the era of "the woke" telling these stories can be problematic for your future employment. Working in the civilian workforce is very different from what we're used to. You're not surrounded by like-minded people you understand how funny it is to have a crack head try and make a police report for a drug deal rip-off at 3 am. Some….may even take offense to it. Yea I know…

If you're leaving law enforcement through retirement, moving on, or through some other reason I would offer you this advice when it comes to telling awesome "Cop stories". Know your audience, it's better to error on the side of caution. Gauge your level of war stores. Remember that these folks think that a "routine" traffic stop is a Michael Bay action thriller. A lot of them can't mentally wrap their heads around old Sally's three legs stabbing her husband with a chicken bone in a meth-induced rage.

Depending on the next profession that you've chosen these stories can also be of great benefit to you. It shows you're experienced with dealing with some crazy shit or gives you credibility with your new peers. Some of our crazy fucked up stories add credibility to what type of experience we bring and that we've been through some crazy shit. Again, you need to know your audience and use it in the right context.

In today's cancel culture "Cop stories" can easily offend a melting snowflake. Human Resources in a lot of companies and government agencies don't find our humor very funny and are typically not very forgiving.

I was talking to a fan of our podcast about his indoctrination back into the civilian workforce. He lasted three weeks before being shown the door. It wasn't because he couldn't do the job, instead it was not adhering to the advice in this book. His first week at the new job everyone in the office discovered that he was a retired cop. For some, this didn't sit well especially after the dumpster fire a few years our profession had. The employees at his former job asked him questions about police use of force and it went down a rabbit hole about George Floyd.

Yep, I know what you're thinking. He took the bait and went down that road. Not only did he go down that road he double down with "If it was me" scenarios. As you could imagine this didn't sit well with his peer and ultimately was asked to leave. Fucked up? Yes, but remember that you're in the civilian world now. A different set of rules in the workforce. It's about the comfort of a select few versus logic. Sound familiar?

Aside from your new place of employment you need to be cautious with stories with your family. If you were like me you typically shared mild to G-rated stories throughout your law enforcement career. After leaving law enforcement I found myself sharing crazy shit with my family. My kids who are 19 and 16 were old enough to understand the stories but I found that my stories were exposing them to things they didn't need to be exposed to. On the other hand, it also let my kids know that the time I spent in law enforcement wasn't all donuts and coffee. In a way it made them realize that all the missed holidays and special events were worth something because I was out there doing things to help people or keep people safe. The stories that upset them is hearing about the abuse from the public or worse yet the command staff in my former agency.

 I remember having my kids on my podcast and listening to them tell that all the things that I protected them from they were fully aware of. They told me that hearing stories with my cop buddies gave them a sense of what I was going through and that they wanted to ask for more details but didn't know how to. I call this collateral storytelling It's when you start telling war stories in an earshot of family You don't think they hear it, but they do. The only difference is they hear the condensed version and they don't get the closure or explanation. Over long periods this causes trauma or jadedness. We see this a lot with cop kids. They are raised around the war stories and get a very different sense of society and in some cases grow up very suspect or jaded. I know in both of my kids this is a definite reality. My kids are very suspect suspicious at first and will tend to be reserved with people. In some ways, I like that, but in another way, I can see that my negativity and jadedness have transferred to my kids. If I could go back and do it again I would have tried to shelter my kids from that.

It's part of the job right? We can tell cop stories for days but struggle with telling family stories at work. A lot of times in law enforcement family stories typically go, "Doing anything good this weekend?", "Yea, my wife has us going to this fucking pumpkin patch. So how crazy was that fucking homicide yesterday bro?". Am I right? In some ways, it's a defense mechanism to block out the family during the shift. Don't think about what you're sacrificing for the job. Don't worry you're not alone, I did it and many others do.

A major piece of advice is don't live in those stories and let them dictate how you live the rest of your life. Make new stories with your family or about new things that you're finally able to do. The stories are the past.

Chapter 5

"Leadership PTSD"

This was a major adjustment for me leaving law enforcement. Leadership in law enforcement is like no other profession, not even the military. Leadership in law enforcement is not really leadership but rather a dictatorship mixed with a cult mindset.

Early on when you're hired in law enforcement is when the cult mindset starts. Law enforcement is one of the hardest professions to get into and eliminates more people than it welcomes in. Because of that, you have a sense of allegiance and debt of gratitude to the organization. So much so that we typically will put up with an incredible amount of abuse and overworking because of it.

Law enforcement leadership especially lately is typically made up of company men and women who will cut each other's throats to get just a sliver of praise from the chief or sheriff. A lot of times you're hot for a little bit till someone else comes along and does something better or newer. This creates a dangling carrot mentality in law enforcement. You're always chasing that carrot to eat rather than saying, "Fuck it, I can buy my own fucking carrot!".

In law enforcement the moment you become self-aware or that something isn't right is the day you're out. There is nothing more than law enforcement agencies hate than an officer that becomes aware that the place is fucked up, being run into the ground, or that knee pads get you what you want. This is where the cult reference comes in. Just like in a cult the leader doesn't want anyone infiltrating or rocking the establishment. This can cause other members to grow a brain and realize that shit is fucked up and potentially leave.

You always see this in a law enforcement promotional process. Typically factions stick together and will help elevate each other to keep the fucked up train running full steam ahead and never helping the officer who's busting his/her ass trying to get promoted. That person is a threat to the establishment.

Now, take the civilian world of leadership. One of the major adjustments for me was the difference between law enforcement leadership and the civilian world.

The first week at my new job I was required to be on a video conference call. Like any new job, you get your email and credentials to log in to many different programs. At the time of the conference call my log on wasn't working and I couldn't attend. Having come from law enforcement this gave me major anxiety about being in trouble. I feverishly emailed my boss explaining the situation and tried to resolve the issue to get on the call. My boss simply texts me "Ok, Don't worry about it". In cop world, this typically means, "Wait till this call is over and I'm going to light you the fuck up".

I waited for the call to be over and anxiously called my boss apologizing over and over again. My boss said to me, "Nick, seriously it's just a call. We don't stress out over that stuff. What did they do to you at the police department?". I had to take a deep breath and realize that I'm in a different world now. I'm working in a professional environment now. Think about that... Law enforcement is supposed to be such an elite profession but we can't act professionally.

Over the course of many months, this type of leadership PTSD reared its ugly head time and time again. I found that leadership has a very different meaning in the civilian world that would greatly improve the quality of life in law enforcement.

In the civilian world, your input is taken in and considered for the common goal of helping the company or agency. Everyone has one goal in mind which is to get it done and make the company achieve its goal. This is done by utilizing each person's strengths without reservation or hidden agenda.

In law enforcement, the goal is to get it done but to get as many of my ideas in the project as possible and make the chief or sheriff aware that, "I" came up with those ideas. It's a crack of horse shit and the reason why we have so many fucked up policies that make no sense or it takes three months to get one memorandum approved.

Law enforcement has become so political with leadership that it runs as dysfunctional as the government. The amount of lobbying that's done to get a policy passed or to assess punishment for an internal investigation is astounding.

The civilian work world doesn't care about ridiculous policies to contain its employees or regulate what they do on their off time. They are too busy pushing the mission forward and having faith in their employees to do the right thing rather than bet on them doing the wrong thing. If something needs to be done and it benefits the mission or company it's enacted by saying, "Do it". They don't waste time making employees write memorandums in hopes they get frustrated and give up on an idea. Or, have five people change the memorandum so it doesn't even closely resemble what you had in mind.

Does the civilian work world have leadership issues? Of course, it does, every place has "leaders" that you wish were locked in a cage with tigers. What separates the two is the level of disconnect from its employees.

Mental health has always and will always be a major issue for me. A lot of our law enforcement mental health issues are caused by poor leadership. You have no idea how coming into work and working for a toxic person can force you to do things that you would never expect of yourself or others. There's a reason our suicide rate is through the roof within law enforcement. Leadership is a major contributor. Now, look at the civilian world and companies like Verizon, Apple, and other major companies. Their focus is internal customer service and the well-being of their employees. If your internal customers are unhappy the external customer will feel the effects. The product that's put out by your employees is affected when they are unhappy or treated poorly.

Why is that accepted in law enforcement? If we have a major problem and our product in law enforcement is not quality why are our CEOs held accountable? Instead, we pass them around like a peace pipe. Once one terrible chief is done destroying an agency they move on to another. Years on the job are looked at as a badge of honor instead of looking at what they've done to project future leaders, improve morale, or mental health.

Leadership is severely lacking in law enforcement with no end in sight. You just don't realize how fucked up it is until you put down the kool-aid cup for a minute and become self-aware.

Chapter 6

"Lunch"

Lunch? I know, when you read the chapter title you probably couldn't figure out where I was going with it. Hear me out and It'll all make sense.

When leaping from law enforcement to civilian life, lunch is probably one of the biggest culture shocks other than going to the bathroom without having to take off a million pieces of equipment.

Lunch as a law enforcement officer is typically made up of cramming McDonald's or something really unhealthy into your mouth in between calls for service. If you're one of those very rare disciplined people you're a meal preparer. If you are, I salute you and your commitment.

As cops, we've accepted the fact that no meal will ever be hot or come with ketchup or hot sauce without spilling it on your vest or shirt. We accept the fact that most meals are in a crammed cruiser hidden from the public. Even being parked in a parking lot miles away from civilization we still seem to attract that one idiot who comes walking from behind our cruiser and says, "Hey officer, did I startle you? I wanted to tell you about a drug deal I saw last month around the corner". This all while you hold a sandwich in your hand and look at this dummy with a blank stare.

We know where to eat and where not to eat. We judge restaurants by whom we arrested that works there or calls for service we've been on there. We remember what kitchens look like going on that late-night alarm call and by the condition of the place when no one is in it.

One of the reasons we retreat to a vacant parking lot or hidden is because the moment you break your rule of eating in a restaurant on duty and in uniform the same thing happens. You're sitting at the table eating a great meal and a group walks in and there's always that one clown that grabs his friend and yells out, "I got him! He's right here! You're in trouble now man!". Happens a million times and every time it's happened to me I wanted to throw a ketchup bottle at the person's head. One it's not funny and two let me enjoy my meal…

If it's not the king of comedy at the restaurant it's this scenario that is probably the one I hated the most. You're minding your own business eating your Chipotle and the table next to you has kids and Karen. One of the kids is anti Chipotle and ain't having it. Karen say's, "If you don't eat I'm going to have this police officer arrest you". This gets under my skin and I've had to set a few Karens right. Don't fucking make us the bad guy… Why are you making the next serial killer hate us? Parent you asshole!

These are just a few examples of the fun times of being a cop and trying to eat a meal on duty if you're lucky. A lot of times a shift has you consuming energy drinks, snacks, and lots of fast food. On midnights your body is in constant shock because it can't figure out why you're having dinner in the morning and breakfast in the evening.

We become custom to carrying these on-duty meal habits into our off-duty life. Our families learn that we don't like going out to eat in public and if we do it's isolated to the back of the restaurant with our back to the wall. My family after a while stopped asking to go out on days off and if by slim chance we did it resulted in me being in a bad mood through the whole meal while I scanned the room for people I might know.

When I left law enforcement this part of "normal" took a lot to get used to. I was no longer a slave to calls for service and my opportunity to eat was wide open. It didn't help that one of my triggers for stress and anxiety was to eat, and eat I did.

Once I had no uniform or vest to shove my dad body into the flood gates opened. When I left law enforcement which you can read about in "Police Mental Barricade" and "Dark Side of the blue line" I had an enormous amount of anger about the way I was excommunicated with very little physical activity. I was writing and podcasting like crazy which required zero physical exertion. I was using food as a crutch or not eating at all and then slamming a gigantic meal at the end of the day.

I traded a police cruiser for a podcast studio and started to replace bad habits with worse habits. It took a long time for me to want to go out in public and eat. What once was my pride about being a cop was now what kept me from going out. Instead of worrying about running into someone I arrested, I worried about running into someone from my old agency. I didn't have fear, I feared for them to run into me. I was out of the job and no longer had to hold back telling a commander that they were cancer or a terrible cop that they shouldn't even be allowed to be a dog catcher.

I remember one time shortly after leaving my department and the Roll Call Room Podcast was at its peak I went to a local Mexican restaurant. I don't know why but I had this overwhelming feeling that something bad was about to happen. I remember doing a weapon bump on my hip like I've always done and it wasn't there anymore. No one knew it at the time but I started to panic and tear up because it had hit me that it was all gone. Everything I worked hard for and sacrificed was summed up at that moment. I had no job, I had no plan, and if something happened like I've imagined a million times I couldn't even protect my family. It didn't matter at that moment who was right and who was wrong, the only thing that was for sure was I wasn't a cop anymore and that sucked.

My wife for a long time walked on eggshells when we went out to restaurants and would always ask, "You ok?" and I would rip her head off every time. That day at the restaurant when everything was hitting me I looked over at her and just wanted to hear her say it again. Instead, the woman I've been with for over 25 years asked, "What's wrong?". I don't know what my face looked like at the time she asked but I know inside I was screaming, "HELP". Instead, the only words I could get out were, "I'll be ok". I wasn't but it took a meal outside of law enforcement to make me realize the magnitude of how very different my future is going to be.

Over the course of the next few months, I learned how to relax during meals and took major steps to stop living in heightened alertness at restaurants with my family. In one instance my wife and I went to a restaurant and she automatically made her way to the chair with its back to the door. I surprised her by saying, "I'll sit there, you've had my back this long I think you can watch it for another hour". Did I look back every time the door opened, yea of course but it was a step towards normal.

The point is that "Lunch" is probably the most normal thing that's not normal for us in law enforcement. We don't get to back a Transformer's lunch box with hot pockets and clock out for a meal. It's something that you don't realize that you've given up because it's such a small thing. It's so small that you lose it without missing it, but it's something that when you leave law enforcement your thankful to get back.

If you're still in law enforcement and doing the things I spoke about, take a moment and evaluate what it's doing to you, your health, and most of all the loved ones around you. Remember your bull shit is their bull shit and anytime you can cut some of it out, do it.

Chapter 7

"Regret, failure, and repeat"

I'm no expert on what to do when you decide to leave law enforcement, but I can definitely tell you what not to do to avoid regret, failure, and repeating your mistakes.

The most important thing is to leave law enforcement before it affects your mental health, family, and potential to find other employment. Like I said at the start of this book, only you can make the decision to leave law enforcement. Many people will give you advice on leaving or staying. On Facebook, law enforcement groups debate this very topic a lot. Many will tell you, "stick with it, it'll get better", "Get out, the job is dead". I can tell you from experience that the worst thing you can do is leave when you're not ready or you listen to people who have no vested interest in your well-being.

In 2019, I left the Alexandria City Police Department after so many reasons but mostly because of my chief's inability to handle a workplace harassment claim I made against a commander. I asked some of my peers if I was making the right choice and all of them said, "Yea! Screw this place". Before I accepted a position with another agency in a civilian position I gave very little thought to what I was getting myself into. My wife was very supportive and allowed me to make the decision but she encouraged me to leave.

My physical health from stress and dealing with my department's lack of empathy towards my complaint drove me to panic attacks and on one occasion I thought of a heart attack. Luckily it wasn't but it made me rush to a hasty decision.

This decision was reinforced by my horrible exit interview with my chief. I talk about this in my first book so I don't want to repeat the same substance but he made me feel insignificant and basically dismissed me like a piece of shit. This only made my bad decision feel more right when it wasn't.

Over a year since that exit incident, I only recently realized why it was the wrong time for me to leave law enforcement. I wasn't done. Plain and simple the fight was still in me. I still had some good mileage in me, the only problem was it wasn't in a uniform. My podcast, training classes, and books wouldn't exist without making that terrible decision.

Over my 20 year career in law enforcement I've made a lot of bad decisions and each time I was able to learn enough not to repeat them. In this instance, repeat and repeat I would do a lot. I've never walked away from what I knew was right and never ever allowed a bully to get the best of me or anyone else. Even if that meant standing up for what I believe is right and it would cost me from wearing another shield again.

After I left the Alexandria City Police Department I realized pretty quickly that I made a terrible mistake. The major reason was going to work for a major police department and being the supervisor of background investigations in recruiting. This might sound like a pretty awesome job and you would be right if it wasn't for working for a civilian Director who believed that everyone can be a cop and murderers can be forgiven enough to wear a uniform. I shit you not… My integrity was far too important to me for the title and pay.

The most humbling experience of my life is going back to my old department and having my Sergeant rank taken away and being a patrol officer again. Embarrassing? Yes, but it taught me a lot of things. I was able to see things from the ground up and understand the rank and file more. It felt good to have a lot of knowledge and experience on a shift where none existed. It also put a target on me because I became very outspoken about the lack of leadership within the agency.

When I started my podcast my original co-host and I was the head of the union. We thought we were untouchable and I believed it because at the time he was my friend. Shit, he was like a brother to me and I attended his wedding.. When it came to trusting someone he was someone that I confided in and told things to which was a major mistake and later would end in war.

When my department brought me up on charges a week before the end of my probation (Yea that's not retaliation) it was clear that the writing was on the wall. Where was my best friend and co-host? Running for the hills and covering his ass. When he broke off from the podcast and started his own I wasn't happy but I dug deep and supported him. When he started to reach out to our old guests and it was clear that he was trying to re-create The

Roll Call Room Podcast was when I put my foot down. Did I do it right? Probably not looking back but what shouldn't have happened was going to my wife and sharing every dirty secret I trusted him with. Yea.. that really happened and caused collateral damage that's unimaginable. In full transparency, I was making a lot of mistakes and being very self-destructive, but you never cross that line.

At one point I was putting fires out all around me. My home life was a disaster thanks to me, my kids hated being around me, I had no job, and about to lose my house and car. Instead of buckling up and attacking the problem, I threw myself into the podcast more. I replaced one addiction with another.

While I was dealing with all of this crashing on me I was dealing with assholes from my former agency calling me a thief and a liar without even knowing the real story. These are the same assholes that I covered shit up for or I witnessed do far worse. I found it ironic that the Captain who interrogated me also notarized power of attorney while the person was passed out on pain medication on her death bed. A felony in Virginia, but I'm the criminal…

I watched as friends or people I thought were friends make memes and post them on social media about me, but forgot that everyone has a dirty secret and no one is clean. It didn't matter because I wasn't in the club anymore. What I didn't realize at the time was that I was now in a more elite club called the "Fallen angels club".

A group of cops were forced out or fucked over because they stopped drinking the kool-aid. I traveled around and discovered that my story wasn't isolated to the Alexandria City Police Department. Iowa has the same positional equity leaders/commanders that would cut your throat in a heartbeat. These were some of the realistic people I've ever met.

I learned that a lot of these law enforcement non-profits geared towards helping with mental health are bullshit. They have events and conferences to jerk each other off but can't give you one example of someone that they saved from committing suicide. They have zero credibility and when they speak to the rank and file of any agency are immediately tuned out. Organizations that take in large sums of money and pay themselves salaries are a problem. When I was going through my shit with my agency and attempted to commit suicide I didn't even know any of these organizations existed. Why? Well because they don't utilize what's right in front of them… US! When I asked to speak at conferences or on video sessions I was told in a nice way to fuck off because they had some fucking Ph.D. or founder of some bullshit organization. It made me sick to watch as officers were committing suicide and these organizations' best response to it was making graphics to get more donations.

Don't get me wrong, there are some really great police organizations out there that are doing great things, but your great things are judged by the people you're trying to help, not by the number of donations you secure.

The mistake I made and made repeatedly was trusting those organizations were honest and weren't using the fan base we had to further their donations. I spent a lot of time thinking that the more I promoted them the more people we were helping which was so incorrect.

These books and the podcast saved more lives than 20 years of law enforcement or any "non-profit". That's a statement that I don't take lightly and anyone that knows me can tell you that I've never been in it for that. Do I regret the collateral damage created because of things I've done? Absolutely! If I could go back and undo certain things or terminate relationships with people that my wife told me were toxic I would. What I don't regret and never will is standing up to some of the leadership in law enforcement that has destroyed this profession.

The biggest thing to take away from this chapter is to know when your story is over in law enforcement. Know when to hang it up and don't be ashamed of it. We're in a profession that not everyone can do it because it takes a unique professional to deal with order and chaos. Too many times we allow this profession to define our existence and think by walking away we lose our identity. Trust me this was a major struggle for me and continues to be. Each day that goes by it gets less painful how I was excommunicated and my anger towards the people who did its slowly turns into pity for them and that I was that much of a threat to them. The officers at the Alexandria City Police Department have no idea how what I did to get a terrible chief removed will benefit them for years to come. They have no idea the number of hours I spent submitting Freedom of Information Act requests for copies of emails, schedules, and meeting notes to prove countless instances of lying and corruption. They have no idea that while the chief was smiling and waving at them he was secretly fucking them all while the unions sat back and sucked him off. I had zero vested interest in that place but still stick to my oath which was to protect and serve from enemies foreign and domestic. Something that a lot of commanders in that place forgot how to do.

In the end, it all boils down to living with what your narrative is. If you're comfortable with being someone who jumps on social media and bullies people because you're a fraud then that's what you'll always be. It takes someone whom to stand up to that and takes the fall out, takes the punches, and knows that it may cost you some things but it isn't everything. This job, yes job, won't pay you back for those memories. Don't live through pictures.

Chapter 8

"Defining your existence"

The longer you're in law enforcement the harder it is for some to define your existence with life after the badge. A lot of retirees struggle with this and is one of the leading causes of mental health issues.

Prior to leaving law enforcement, I couldn't understand why this was. I would watch retirees or people or left the profession struggle with defining their existence in the public world and think to myself, "It's not that hard, just move on". I was seriously naive and wrong with my thought process. This job sinks its claws into you and you buy into something that no one else can understand.

For me it was pride. Pride in waking up each day and knowing that I was doing something I always wanted to do and very few have the balls to do. I knew that even on the worst day's sleep or if my personal home life was not good that I was going to a job that needed me. I knew that I was going to do some good that day.

I always go changed at work and took suiting up in my uniform like preparing for battle. I always took pride in how my uniform looked and making sure my boots were shinned. I took pride in representing my agency as professionally as I could. I'd listen in the locker room as some would bitch and complain about working and the internal politics. Believe it or not, I never subscribed to locker room court. I stayed away from airing grievances publicly. Mostly because we had scum bag commanders who would creep around and record conversations or hold personal grudges from locker room talk.

When I entered roll call I tried to keep it light-hearted because this could be the last time we all saw each other. As a Sergeant, this was a major battle with some command staff. Everyone has that one Captain, Lieutenant, or Chief that comes into roll call and fucks morale up. We had one Captain who would come in and aside from saying, "Umm" every other word was the fucking king of gloom and doom. This guy was a shit-beat cop who mastered taking processes and got promoted off fucking his troops over. Yea, you know that kind of commander. He would come into roll call and say shit like, "Hey, last night an officer was ambushed in NYC. Let's watch the video before you hit the street". I would just look at this clown and remember working for him when I was an officer and think about how much of an asshole he was then and nothing has changed.

Even with dealing with idiots like that, I loved being part of the machine. I had a purpose and at the end of the shift, I felt fulfilled. Good shift, bad shift it didn't matter. When I left it was like the rug pulled out from under me. The first week or two because of the way I was forced out I spent in a fog. Shit, the first three days I didn't get out of bed. I was lost.. Anyone that knows me knows that I am by far my own worst critic. I beat myself up for days about how much different things could have been. Was the cause worth losing everything over?

Looking back now I still can't answer that. Is the cause worth it? In some ways, it's allowed me to get books like this out and into your hands. It's a reminder to people like you that your department isn't special. The Alexandria City Police Department isn't just located in Virginia. It's in Texas, California, and all over the world. Everyone has that asshole commander or chief. Everyone has a tactical Tommy in their department. But we go with it for the good of the job.

When you leave the job that all disappears. This is going to sound odd but you'll miss it to an extent. I don't miss looking over my shoulder wondering when I was going to get stabbed in the back by one of my commanders or co-workers, but I miss the pride. I miss the little things. I miss going to the dry cleaners and picking up my uniforms and feeling a sense of pride. I miss the mundane nights of being a cop. The smell of 0300 in October reminds me of peace. Stupid stuff like smoking cigars with co-workers when the gates of hell close long enough to joke around and act normal.

What I don't miss is having Thanksgiving dinner in my cruiser and trying not to think about my family and how I miss them. Or, riding in the new year going from noise complaint to noise complaint and watching people enjoying themselves while you sit on the sideline of life.

After leaving law enforcement all of these good or bad memories create a void. Some fill these voids with bad habits like drinking or gambling. This is the dangerous road a lot of former LEO's go down and not a lot of support or intervention after you leave the job. A lot of these mental health programs or organizations focus on current law enforcement and turn a blind eye to the ones who leave the profession. Honestly, those are the ones you need to worry about. When you on the job you know somethings wrong with you or know you have hints of Post Traumatic Stress Disorder (PTSD) but it's stuffed down so you can do the job every day. When you leave the job it slams you in the face. Your brain has nothing else to worry about so it brings up that homicide you worked or dead baby case and wants you to deal with it.

Some of these "Non-profits" talk a good game about helping LEO's but in reality, they are spinning their wheels. I've made suggestions to get some of them more engaged with law enforcement and add credibility so folks are more likely to utilize resources and it's fallen on deaf ears. Fundraising is not raising awareness..

A lot of the time after law enforcement is determining or analyzing the amount of dedication and effort you put into the job. Was it worth it? That answer can only come from you, but I can tell you that no time was wasted on your hard work. The time spent away from family you can never get back but don't take that as wasted time or time that wasn't spent doing good.

I struggled and continue to struggle with this in my own personal life. I joined law enforcement when my kids were really young. I missed a lot of their lives growing up and now that I'm out of the job they're all grown up. At times I wonder how things would be if I would have had an office job and off on weekends. What would their lives look like now? Then, I also look at the valuable lessons they've learned from me being a cop. I know that raising two daughters that no one will ever be able to bullshit them into doing something they don't want to. I know that they always exercise caution when someone is "selling" them something. I know a lot of non-cop parents whose kids could be convinced the world is flat and that water is dry. I'd rather have my kids self-aware and not some snowflake who can easily be conned into a cause without knowing the truth. I'm proud of my kids for always seeking the facts and truth rather than going with the crowd.

If you don't have kids and you're out of law enforcement now, take the opportunity to adjust your mindset before having kids.

The most important thing about defining your existence after law enforcement is to have an existence. Leaving the job leaves an incredible void in your life without a doubt, but it can and should be filled with a life that you set forward for yourself. What did you enjoy doing before the job? What hobbies did you "no longer" have time for? Get back to those. Pick up a hobby you've been putting off. Learn an instrument to play. Reach out to podcasts and share your journey or stories.

Don't replace the job with the job! Many former first responders leave the job and jump into volunteering. It's pretty much like a cocaine addict replacing cocaine with alcohol. "I'll just volunteer a little", turns into now full-time volunteering just to get a taste of that adrenaline or be around the clown and circus. Don't do it. You either was a clean break or no break at all.

Your existence is what you make of it folks. The job was fun and the roller coaster was fun. All the certificates, plaques, and awards don't buy back a moment of time with your family. Remember that.

Chapter 9

"It's a bad car crash"

By

Logan Campbell

My law enforcement career started early. Around 1988. I was born into a police family in central Indiana. So many memories from my childhood are full of having to be quiet in the mornings because dad was sleeping upstairs or us celebrating holidays with him in uniform.

I never thought anything about it, though. It was just normal life for me and my brother. It was a day in and day out cop-life. The SWAT callouts. The off-duty traffic stops with me in the front seat. The weekends spent at the range. It encircled who we were as a family and was our normal. He was a firearms instructor and being the avid gun-loving kid I was, I would go with him and just hang out at the range. Listening to other cops talk to one another. Learning the lingo. I was hooked early.

My dad was a cop for over 30 years. That's a long time to be in any profession, let alone one as potentially mentally and physically damaging as police work. I am honestly not too sure if it damaged him at all. He started in the '90s, which was an era of policing that sort of "Lives in infamy." Thankfully, working for a semi-rural county sheriff's office, the big city type policing didn't really occur there, to my knowledge.

I guess I wanted to be a cop when I was younger, but honestly, I'm not sure when I got the itch to do it. As I said, I always loved the cool part of the job: the firearms training, the defensive tactics, you know, the movie shit. I had no idea how much of that stuff very rarely happens on a day-to-day basis for cops in the midwest. Much like the majority of America, I assumed it was like the wild west every day. Hostage negotiations, shootouts, and vehicle chases.

It wasn't until I got a little older that I realized policing was more about service than protection, most of the time.

And by most of the time, I would venture to say about 65% of the time you are serving in one way or another. Whether it's taking a theft report from someone who has no serial numbers or anything for the $12,000 worth of power tools that they left unlocked and were stolen overnight or solving a dispute between neighbors about who is cutting their lawn too short. You are always serving in one way or another.

Then the other 35% is spent on the protected side of the coin, but even that isn't what you think it would be. It's not about saving the bus full of nuns and orphans from the rampaging wild-man down the street or whatever. It's more about being called to a domestic disturbance, sneaking up to the house, and actually witnessing, through the windows, the male punch the female in the face. Then, going inside, fighting with the resisting male to get him in handcuffs, only to be struck in the back by his wife because "He said he was sorry and he doesn't need to go to jail." I know it's happened to so many cops, but it was always so shocking to me when it did.

Now obviously, this is not even the tip of the spear that is law enforcement in the United States, but you get what I'm saying. We could get into proactive policing, traffic stops, and all other things, but the majority of the folks reading this probably already know about that shit.

I'm here to talk about when I got out and why.

I went to college for telecommunications. I started my college career in August of 2007. I wanted to be involved in some form of media communication: radio, television, anything. Then, once I got into it, they told me it was going to be a 6-year program because it was so full and there just weren't enough teachers.

So, I moved on. I changed my major to physical education. I was a year into that when I slowly realized that I hate other people's children. Don't get me wrong, if I know you and your kids, then you know I got love and respect for you. But when they unleashed about 27 third graders on me to "teach them how to play basketball," I knew right then and there that teaching was not for me.

So, like any good student of the "No child left behind era," I knew that I had to pick something to do with my life. College was a MUST and was damn near required to be successful in life and if I didn't graduate with a degree in something related to my lifetime profession then I was a failure to my parents, my country, and anyone else who happened to meet me in the future.

What a line of bullshit. So, I decided to do what any rational college-aged kid would do with only 2 years left in college, I majored in Criminal Justice and Criminology and went into the family business: law enforcement. If you are considering being a street cop, do not get a degree in criminal justice or anything like it. Don't waste your time or your money. That degree did not help me at all when it came to getting a job or even on the job at all. Unless you are planning to go federal, major in business, or something worthwhile, so you've got a plan B.

Anyway, I started working part-time in the jail as a correctional officer on my weekends. My eyes were opened to what policing is actually like, and that was just from the inside of the jail. I got to witness how evil some people can be, how

CRAZY some people can be, and how sad some situations actually are.

In the middle of working part-time, I had to do an internship for school. So, I chose to do it at the jail where I was already working. During that, I did get to do some ride alongs and witness the street work of the deputies. It was during this time that I witnessed my first death.

I won't go into enormous detail about it here. It's a long story for another time. In the short story, I was a 21-year-old intern rolling up to a semi-tractor engulfed in flames with an experienced road deputy. Inside the semi was the driver, screaming for his life because he was burning alive, and there was nothing we could do to save him. Within the first 30 minutes of my internship, I witnessed a person burn to death. My scarring started early in my career and I didn't even know it.

So after graduating and working part-time, I got offered a full-time position inside the jail. And then, after a few years, I got offered a position as a deputy sheriff. So I got to go to the academy, went through field training, and was then released on the road out into the wild. It was just me, 2 other deputies, and a 425 square mile county that needed policing.

For the next several years, I made some of the best friends I have ever had, and still have to this day. We fought together, bled together, and laughed together. It was what you'd expect from law enforcement.

But, we also experienced things that most cops do as well. Scarring, traumatizing events that will never leave our minds. Like that time in 2015 when I was almost killed during a pursuit. Guy came across two lanes of a county road and tried to hit me while I laid out stop sticks. I stepped out of the way and he hit my SUV at 104 mph. The guys joked about it later, they called me "The Matador " because I side-stepped the Mercury Mountaineer as it came barreling towards me.

His driver's side mirror grazed my shoulder. It was close.

Talk about mental scars. I went through some therapy for that one. Luckily, the department that I was working for offered me a week off work and mandated I go and speak with a therapist about the incident. It was beneficial, to say the least.

Shortly after, I transferred up north to another department in northern Indiana. We saw an opportunity there and my family and I decided that we needed a change. So we packed up our life and moved up to northern Indiana where I started police work as a patrolman for a municipality. My retirement started over. In Indiana, the Sheriff's office is not on the public employee retirement system, like a municipal police officer is, so when I left the sheriff's office, my retirement date started over. I was still young, so I didn't think anything about it.

I took the oath and pledged to protect the city with everything I had, up to and including my life. I then sat down in a 2011 Chevy Impala, went through field training, and was released for police work. It was like I stepped back in time. This was in 2016, mind you.

So, I made the best of it. I did my job, policed the community, and even got involved in several different opportunities within the department. Honor guard, taser instructor, field training officer. I was feeling really good about it all. That is until I wasn't anymore.

It was somewhere in the year 2018 when things really started hitting me. I know my mental health wasn't the best. I knew I had some underlying issues from, ya know, almost being murdered and all that. I was working nights, not sleeping the best, filling that "void" in my head with chewing tobacco, working out, and video games.

I was told when I first started in policing that the "Two things that will get a cop in trouble are a woman's ass and a whiskey glass."

Well, I luckily don't drink to excess, very rarely as it is, and my wife and I had a great marriage. I didn't rely on alcohol or cheating to "cope with the job." I know that is a vice that a lot of cops deal with.

Luckily, none of my vice's had really caused me any issues.

I got a text one day from a friend down south and all it read was "Hey, call me."

This was way out of the ordinary, so I called him. His first words were "Hey - Pickett's shot - bad." He told me that one of my friends and former co-worker at my old department had been shot during a pursuit, and probably was not going to survive.

Cue the world spinning effect.

I had attended lots of funerals and stood to watch at many caskets in my time in the Honor Guard unit, but I never once thought about having to do it for a friend. I opened my eyes.

Then, as the years continued, my kids started growing up, as they do, and noticing when I wasn't at home or at the ballet. I was working the afternoon shift, so my shift was always in the middle of everything.

To top it all off, we were short on manpower at work, so we could only take time off if we traded with another guy. It got rough. When it came to overtime we had the option of either taking it in cash or taking it in banked time off hours. I always took it in comp time. My wife worked, so we didn't *need* the extra money, so I took the time. I figured I spent enough time there as it was, I wanted to spend more time away from it all. The guys would always laugh at me because as soon as I had enough hours to take a full day off, I would. It was so relieving to me to not have to go to work and deal with people.

That was when I started noticing it more and more. I used to love this job. As a kid, I wanted nothing more than to be a cop. And now, as a cop, I wanted nothing more than to have a day off from being a cop. The turntables had turned.

Then, 2020 happened. I know I don't have to go into all the lockdowns, the riots, the looting. All the bullshit. But yeah, 2020 happened to policing.

I always say that the year 2020 is like Rocky V, it happened, it was real, but we just choose to not talk about it any more than we have to.

Maybe it was the riots. Maybe it was being called a racist on calls more often than usual. Maybe it was my friend's murder still haunting me. Maybe it was my own close call with death hanging around. Maybe it was being told to "Go sit in a parking lot and do nothing" for 6 months in 2020 and then to be told that we had a "Shift goal" of "traffic contacts" to make and that my evaluation within the department would be based on how many "contacts" I got. "Maybe it was my kids telling me to "Be safe and don't die."

I will honestly never know exactly what it was that pushed me over the edge. I had thought a lot about leaving law enforcement, but I had no idea what I would do. I had a bachelor's degree in criminal justice, my entire professional career was law enforcement-related, and I knew nothing outside of law enforcement. I had literally been born and raised around it.

It scared me to think about leaving it, but I knew I did NOT want to spend another 15 years doing it. Day after day, the thought of staying in for more than a decade made me sick. My mental health was on the decline, and I knew it.

Leadership at the department changed, which then changed the dynamic of how things worked. I was never a numbers guy. I didn't care how many arrests I made. I cared that everyone went home alive. Cops and civilians alike. Do the job, take the calls, make a few stops, write the reports, take some folks to jail.

The usual. But at some point during the last year or so, I noticed that my daily goal changed from "Get an arrest" to "Don't get called into the office." Closed-door meeting after closed-door meeting. They will tell you all day long that their door is "Always open" until they ask you to shut it. Now,

I'm not going to sit here and complain about the asinine reasons as to why I was given a "Coaching session" in those meetings. Maybe that's for another time... But let me tell you this, just because something isn't written the way YOU would write it, does NOT make it wrong. I found myself being excited at the end of a shift, not only because I was going home, but because I didn't get called into the office.

That excitement at the end of the shift slowly turned into stress at the beginning, which then turned into panic attacks before even driving into work.

I can't tell you exactly what it was that bothered me about going in. I could never pinpoint it. It was the culmination of things, all rolled into one giant firehose, that I felt like I was sprayed with day in and day out. A relentless onslaught of stressing over what supervisor was working, were we short-staffed that day, was all of my equipment going to work that day, was I going to be murdered on duty, was I going to be involved in something at work that could possibly put my livelihood in jeopardy all because
I did my job? The list went on and on.

This was a daily thought process for me as I got ready for work and drove in. I was just done. Mentally, physically. I just did not want to do the job anymore. It's so hard to put into words how much I wanted to just turn my gear in and never go back. Leave all the shitty calls and shitty people behind. Just be done.

It was always important to me to have friends outside of the job. Over the years, as policing got "worse" (by worse I mean started to get more and more negative media attention, which then was exacerbated by social media), my friends would always ask me the same question: "What would it take for you to leave law enforcement?" I always gave the same answer: $60,000 a year, good health insurance, and a vehicle." That's all it would take for me to leave it all behind. I feel like it always shocked people to know

I was so quick to provide that answer.

I guess after a few years I fell out of love with the job. It lost its luster for me. I grew up around it, I grew up in it. Hell, I got a college degree in criminal justice. I literally had prepared to be a cop for almost 2 decades. And then suddenly, after a few years of actually doing the job. Seeing all the death. Dealing with the unreasonable. Being spit on, fought with, cursed at, nearly killed.

If someone offered me more than my cop salary to NOT have to deal with that stuff, I would have taken it in a heartbeat. No questions asked. I was just never offered that chance. Of course, I never really looked, until about the spring of 2021.

I'm not quite sure what it was that actually pushed me to the edge, but I was definitely not in a good place during the first few months of 2021. Maybe it was the aftermath or 2020, maybe it was the leadership, maybe it was the job finally getting to me. I'll honestly never know. All I know is, I was having thoughts of suicide. Not suicidal thoughts, but thoughts of suicide. I never really made a plan or thought about how I would do it, it was more "What would happen if I did?"

Now, these thoughts of suicide would make me feel worse than I did before. Not only was I thinking about being dead, but then I would think about what would happen to my kids and my wife and my family. Then I would feel guilty about thinking about wanting "out" of my life. I mean, one of the things I stressed about was dying on duty, and yet I was thinking about taking my own life? It made no sense. I knew I was not in my right mind and I needed to talk to someone.

I had dozens of conversations with my wife Hannah about it all. Throughout our entire marriage, we have known nothing but law enforcement. I was in it before we got together, so all she knew of me was law enforcement. I can safely say that we have had a great marriage, but not without its pitfalls. We've argued, we've yelled at each other, and we dealt with anger and sorrow. But we did it all together. She supported me no matter what, which is more than I can say about a lot of cops in their marriages. I was very lucky to have her.

As my mental health began its spiral down, I found myself becoming more and more impatient with the kids. Losing my temper, raising my voice, and just "needing a minute." She would always suggest I just go take a minute if I was feeling overwhelmed or anything.

I never did. I would just let my mind fill up with impatience and anger. The hell of it was, I wasn't ever angry AT anything. I could never put my finger on it.

I started reading more and more about anxiety and stress and how humans react to it. Signs of an anxiety attack. Some folks shake, hyperventilate, and damn near have heart attacks. Not me. I would find myself staring off into space. I would be standing in the kitchen, looking through the window, lost in my mind. At some point, I would eventually 'Wake up and have no idea how long I'd been there. I was working the afternoon shift, so a lot of my days were spent alone in the house. Once the wife and kids were gone it was just me and my thoughts. It really wasn't helpful at all.

Honestly, I did not intend this chapter to be about this. It's gone far deeper and longer than I expected it to. Allow me to fast forward, to the better part.

I started therapy. After my wife found me down in the basement, alone, in the dark when the rest of my family was upstairs, she told me I needed to see someone. She saw that I was not the same person and it was obvious that it was close to being dangerous.

She told me that I should contact our church and see if there were some resources available to me.

Lucky for me, they have a licensed therapist on staff that I was able to open up to. Marty helped me put words to how I was feeling about the job and how I just didn't want to do it anymore.

I was always told that being a cop "Isn't what we do, it's who we are." That is a lie. This job swallows the real you up and spits another you out if you let it. Unfortunately, I let it do just that.

When you realize it's just a job and is NOT who you are, then you realize how you can move on.

Folks always wonder why it's so tough to leave law enforcement, especially before getting vested. This is how I looked at it - I can either work for another 15 years to get my retirement from the state, and then look for another job as a 48-year-old former cop looking for a high paying job/waiting to pull my pension, OR I could find something else, secure a new job, and just move on. Stop stressing about it and just move on. Why was I so married to the pension anyway? Why was I so married to the job? A job that can kill me, that, according to the media, the majority of America thinks is racist and bad. It just gets old. It's not what it used to be. So I wanted out. I'm still young. In my thirties, I've still got my entire life ahead of me to go and get a new job, start a new career, and just live the rest of my life. So I did just that.

I shopped around and found a local company that was hiring, that paid just as much as my cop salary, plus commission, and I jumped on it. I haven't looked back since. I feel 10lbs lighter. My mental health has never been better. My family life struggled a bit, I will say. But, it was a huge transition going from me being home in the mornings and during the middle of the week to being gone 8-5 Monday through Friday and being home on the weekends. It wasn't easy, and it's still not. This was only July when I left. After nearly 12 years on the job, I washed my hands of it all, and I don't have a single regret. It was interesting to see how everyone else reacted though. Family, friends, and those I called brothers/sisters.

There is this, for lack of a better term, stigma in policing that "If you don't do the full 20, you abandoned the job and the department and you are a piece of shit." At least, that's how I felt by the way some of my "brothers" treated me. It's gonna happen.

And that's okay. The thing to consider the most is how YOU feel about it. Does it feel right to you? If so, then forget everyone else. It's gonna hurt, and you're gonna feel betrayed, but in all honesty, I think some of them felt betrayed, too. They are just too proud to admit it, or just unwilling to. And that's okay. You will lose friends, you will lose "brothers." All that "thin blue line" crap disappears for some when you decide to leave. Par for the course.

Like I said I made some of the best friends I'll ever have when I was on the job. Still to this day they are my brothers. Some of them. But once I left, a lot of them just cut me out. And that's fine. It's gonna happen. I don't hold it against them.

I'm happy with my choice, and I hope they know that.

Wow, this has gone on much longer than I thought it would. I know Nick's books are typically more profanity-laced and sarcastic, but I wanted to just be raw and real. I've poured my thoughts into this in a few hours, over a 2 day period and it comes down to one conclusion for me. I did my time. I served my communities, and it was simply my time to move on. And I'm happy about that. I truly am.

The job gave me some of the best opportunities that life can give. Some of the best life lessons. I tell people now at my new job, these young kids, that if they want REAL life experience if they want to see how people REALLY treat one another, go be a cop for a week. A year. Hell, go do a few ride-alongs. You will see what humanity truly is. I had just seen enough of it.

Being a cop is, ironically, much like driving past a really bad car crash. You want to leave, you want to look away, but for some reason, you just can't do it. You are fixated on the carnage. The mangled, jagged pieces of metal that were once a well-oiled machine hypnotize you to the point of incoherence.

Don't let the swinging watch captivate your attention and avert your eyes from your own health, mental and physical. Keep your eyes on the road and get home safe, otherwise, you are just another distracted driver staring at a bad car crash, until they either give your significant other a folded flag or give you a retirement badge. Either way, there is gonna be another ass in that cruiser 1 week after you're gone.

I'm not advocating for cops to quit. If you still love the job, I'm so proud of you and support you. All I'm trying to do is tell my story and say that "It's okay to be done." The war will go on without you. You served your time, now go live your life.